PRESIDENT DONALD TRUMP

by Joanne Mattern

Content Consultant

Nanci R. Vargus, Ed.D.

Professor Emeritus, University of Indianapolis

Reading Consultant

Jeanne M. Clidas, Ph.D.

Reading Specialist

Children's Press®

An Imprint of Scholastic Inc.

Library of Congress Cataloging-in-Publication Data
A CIP catalog record for this book is available from the Library of Congress.

Produced by Spooky Cheetah Press
Design by Judith Christ-Lafond
Poem by Jodie Shepherd

© 2017 by Scholastic Inc.

Printed in the United States of America   113

1 2 3 4 5 6 7 8 9 10 R 26 25 24 23 22 21 20 19 18 17

Photographs ©: cover Trump: Dan Hallman/Invision/AP Images; cover background, back cover: Zack Frank/Shutterstock, Inc.; 3 top: spawns/iStockphoto; 3 bottom: creisinger/iStockphoto; 4-5: JEFF KOWALSKY/Getty Images; 6: Seth Poppel Yearbook Library; 8: Barton Silverman/The New York Times/Redux; 10-11: AP Images; 12: John Barrett/Zumapress/Newscom; 14-15: Luis Sinco/Getty Images; 16: Sonia Moskowitz/Getty Images; 18: Victoria Arocho/Hasbro Inc./AP Images; 19: Frazer Harrison/Getty Images; 20-21: Michele Sandberg/Getty Images; 23: Mark Wallheiser/Getty Images; 24-25: TIMOTHY A. CLARY/Getty Images; 26-27: Boston Globe/Getty Images; 29: Win McNamee/Getty Images; 30: Orhan Cam/Shutterstock, Inc.; 31 top: Bettmann/Getty Images; 31 bottom: Rob Crandall/Shutterstock, Inc.; 31 center top: TIMOTHY A. CLARY/Getty Images; 31 center bottom: AP Images; 32: Orhan Cam/Shutterstock, Inc.

Maps by Mapping Specialists

Sources:
page 22: Choron, Harry and Sandra. *Money: Everything You Never Knew About Your Favorite Thing to Find, Save, Spend and Covet*. NY. Chronicle Books, 2011. page 252.

TABLE OF CONTENTS

Meet Donald Trump

Donald Trump is a famous **entrepreneur**. He is also a television personality. In 2015, Trump surprised many people when he decided to run for president. In November 2016, he won the election. Donald Trump became the 45th president of the United States.

Donald John Trump was born on June 14, 1946. His family lived in Queens, New York.

When Donald was young, he used to get in trouble in school. His parents sent him to military school. Donald learned discipline. He learned how to be a leader.

This is Donald's senior class picture.

CANADA

New York
(Queens)

New York
(Manhattan)

Washington,
D.C.

UNITED
STATES

MEXICO

MAP KEY

● City where Donald
Trump was born

■ Cities where Donald
Trump lives

*Area
enlarged*

7

Donald poses with his father in 1973.

Taking Care of Business

Donald's father, Fred Trump, built apartment buildings. Donald started working for his dad while he was in college. He graduated in 1968. About three years later, Fred turned his business over to his son. But Donald did not just want to build apartment buildings. He had bigger plans!

New York officials look at Trump's plans for the new Hyatt hotel.

For his first big project, Trump bought an old hotel in New York City. He **renovated** it to make it more modern. The hotel was renamed the Grand Hyatt. The project made Trump famous.

Ivana poses with her three children (left to right), Donald Jr., Ivanka, and Eric.

In 1977, Trump married his first wife, Ivana. They were married for 15 years and have three children.

In 1983, Trump opened Trump Tower in New York City. The 58-story building includes fancy apartments and stores. There is a waterfall in the lobby.

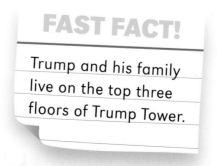

FAST FACT!

Trump and his family live on the top three floors of Trump Tower.

Trump's businesses kept growing. He owned apartment buildings and hotels. He also owned golf courses. There were Trump steaks, clothing, and even bottled water. Some of his businesses were not successful. Many were. Trump would later say his business experience would help him be a strong president.

Trump poses at one of his golf courses.

Marla Maples and Tiffany, in 2013

In 1993, Trump married Marla Maples. They were married for six years.

Trump and Maples have a daughter named Tiffany. She was named after a famous jewelry store. It is right next door to Trump Tower in New York City.

TV Star

In 2004, Trump became the host of *The Apprentice*. The TV show featured people trying to win a job in one of Trump's businesses. They faced many challenges. Every week, Trump would tell the losing contestant, "You're fired!"

FAST FACT!

Trump also wrote several books and had his own board game (left).

Trump, Melania,
and Barron, in 2015

In 2005, Trump married Melania Knauss. She is from Slovenia, a country in central Europe. Their son, Barron, was born in 2006.

In 2008, Trump's TV show changed to *The Celebrity Apprentice*. Celebrities played to win money for charity.

Trump for President

On June 16, 2015, Trump announced he was running for president. He was an unusual choice because he had no experience in **politics**.
Some people liked him because he was an outsider who was new to working in the government.

FAST FACT!

"Perhaps it's time America was run like a business."
— Donald Trump

Trump ran against
Hillary Clinton. She had a lot
more experience in politics.
Clinton had been First Lady of
the United States, as well as a

Trump and Clinton met for three
debates. They each talked about
how they would lead the country.

senator. She had also served as secretary of state under President Barack Obama. In that role, she handled the United States' relationships with other countries.

On November 8, 2016, Americans voted for president. The race was close, but Trump won. Many people were happy. They looked forward to a brand-new government. They hoped for a stronger country.

Trump greets supporters after winning the election.

Donald Trump inspired his supporters to try something new. He promised them a better future. Millions of Americans are counting on him to help improve their lives.

Timeline of Donald Trump's Life

1946

Born on June 14

1971

Takes over his father's company

The Apprentice
first airs

Elected president

2004　　**2015**　　**2016**

Announces presidential
campaign

A Poem About Donald Trump

His buildings reached into the sky.
His businesses just grew and grew.
Then Trump became our president—
people wanted something new.

You Can Be President

Learn how government works.

Listen to other people and learn to share ideas for how to solve problems.

Say what you believe in and work to make your dreams come true.

Glossary

- **entrepreneur** (ahn-truh-pruh-NUR): someone who starts businesses and finds new ways to make money

- **politics** (PAH-li-tiks): activity and discussions involved in governing a country, state, or city

- **renovated** (REN-uh-vay-ted): modernized or restored something to good condition

- **senator** (SEN-uh-tuhr): official elected to make laws

Index

Facts for Now

Visit this Scholastic Web site for more information on President Donald Trump and download the Teaching Guide for this series:

www.factsfornow.scholastic.com

Enter the keywords President Donald Trump

About the Author

Joanne Mattern has written more than 250 books for children. She especially likes writing biographies because she loves to learn about real people and the things they do. Joanne also loves American history and thinks ours is a very interesting nation! She grew up in New York State and still lives there with her husband, four children, and several pets.